A BRIEF HISTORY
OF LOVE

A BRIEF HISTORY

OF LOVE

Poems by Gordon King

Gordon King

To order additional copies of this book, contact:
Xlibris Corporation
1-888-795-4274
www.Xlibris.com
Orders@Xlibris.com
15404

CONTENTS

Dedicated to my lady
Josephine deBeauchamp

A number of these poems were originally published in my book "Oh To Be Loved Like This."

I give grateful acknowledgement to the editors of the following publications in which some of these poems, sometimes in earlier versions, have appeared:

Envoi Magazine
Stoke-on-Trent, England
Doors Magazine
Dorset, England
Asheville Arts Journal
Asheville, North Carolina
Applause Magazine
Tryon, North Carolina
Free Press
Rockland, Maine
The Island Institute
Rockland, Maine
The Camden Herald
Camden, Maine
Annual Anthologies, 1996 and following
The Live Poets Society, Rockland, Maine
Off the Coast Magazine
The Live Poets Society, Rockland, Maine
Weyfarers Magazine
Guildford, England
Anthology, The First Fifteen Years
The Waverley Writers, County Surrey, England

I owe warm thanks to Keith Please of Godalming, Surrey, and to all my fellow poets in his Poetic Pulse meetings for their sharp eyes and ears and steady encouragement. My colleagues in the Waverley Writers group in Surrey have been unfailingly helpful and kind. And from Maine I have been gifted with the perceptive, lucid and supportive comments of poets Ted and Ruth Bookey, George Van Deventer, Emily Breitner and others, old friends and ruthless critics. I am most grateful to all.

Cover art by Josephine deBeauchamp

BY THE SAME AUTHOR

The Family Reunion

Oh To Be Loved Like This

The Blue Balcony

The Hero of Trenton (translation)

But It Does Move

FOREWORD

How does one impose order on poems of love? I've not found it possible. Love insists on its own logic and happily pushes aside my ideas about organization. Therefore I've listed the contents chronologically—thus acknowledging that poems write themselves out of a poet's heart and mind, each work choosing its own hour, its special mood or memory, its particular place.

Those in this collection have one focus in common: a certain redheaded artist who has inspired me to paste a small but bold sign in our window: *A Wild Wacky Wonderful Woman Lives Here!*

SEARCHLIGHT, NEVADA

Sometimes I think of your child trusting face
bright with expectancy and feel new pain,
wondering each time at the kind of love
that could send you away. Stories can't prove
to me that they valued you. Show me again
how they fed you with their hearts, in another place.

Show me the photo. You by that corrupt man,
trusting his arm. He bribed a starving child
with food. He saw you dazzling in the sun
and bought you. Do you cry then for that one?
When he who was to father you defiled
your trust? My dear, I do not think I can.

I can see now into the past's chasm,
the perfidy, the treachery, the cold
rejection by the other man who kept
your mother from you. I know you have wept
for her—but I weep for you, my ten year old,
innocent plaything of their cynicism.

And yet you lived with richness, walked with pride,
practiced your art, stayed at the Savoy,
loved and were loved, made your fierce way,
listened for the laughter, had your say
over half a world, spread your joy
and, miraculously, ended by my side.

THE ART STUDENT

There at the top of the stairs
                against the white wall,
                one of your paintings,
                your *Cold Water Flat,*
Hell's Kitchen, your universe.
Crazy pots in a peeling sink,

and above the sink, a shelf
                piled with junk, more
                pushed to one side
                away from the dripping tap,
and hanging in the place of honor
the key to the john down the hall

which locked the bums out. You gave
                a suicide party, the place
                filled with artists;
                you planned to float
by the window but fell backwards
instead, so returned to the melee

where a guy rushed up. "There
                you are! Thank God!"
                You smiled. "You missed me?"
                "The key!" he shouted.
"I need the key to the john!" You
have always remembered. *Hell's Kitchen.*

THE MEETING

—after Longfellow—
—for Jo—

In the little port of Camden, by the
schooners always waiting, by the inner
harbor's entrance, in the rocky harbor
entrance, sits a man in casual clothing, sits a
man upon a boulder. In one hand he holds a
tablet, in his hand an artist's sketchbook, in
the other hand a paintbrush, dipping into
water colors, copying the scene before him,
measuring the scene in inches. Then behind
him he hears footsteps, definite and female
footsteps, so he turns his head to watch her
come to stand up by his elbow, see the
sketchbook, smile and ask him, "May I look
at what you're doing?" When he grins and
lifts the sketchbook, showing her his honest
effort, she inspects and arches eyebrows,
laughs again, and leaning over, says in
words he will remember, words that make
him watch her closely, "You need help!" He
hands it to her, offers her his work, the
painting.

"You don't mind?" she asks and takes it,
takes the brush, and within minutes has
transformed his novice dabbing to a vivid

rich excitement, to the richness of the
evening. "Who *are* you?" he asks with
feeling. "I'm an *artist*!" she cries, laughing.
She displays a sheaf of paintings, brings her
fresh and merry humor, brings her vivid joy
of living, gives him feelings of deliverance,
gives him colors for his dreaming.

So they walk off into evening, walk into the
Camden sunset, spend an hour in lively
talking, find a restaurant with lobster where
the wine is holy water, where they each
explore the other as her eyes reflect the
candles.Later when they dream the evening,
think of it while flying homeward, think of
pleasure, think of loving, they begin to
dream the future. After months of
corresponding, he flies westward to
the sunset, flies to find this magic woman,
finds her working hard at living, finds her
talking to the ocean, talking to the broad
Pacific, taking him along beside her, laying
out for him her passions, laying out for him
her body.

Warm with magical acceptance, she has love
that is both hunger and a trust as great as
she is, trusting in his basic goodness, and he
answers with emotion, answers with his
deepest longing, ready for a true relating,
ready for a wild adventure, seeing in her all
the freshness, all the yearning lost within
him,

yearning for a loving woman, for a free and
loving woman. In the years they've spent
together, spent in many far adventures, in
the years of tasting freedom, in the
friendship of their loving, what has happened
to their harbor, their enchanting Camden
harbor?

Boats still populate the water, boats of every
shape and rigging, and the days are full of
people, but along the rocky entrance, on a
rocky promontory when the tide is drained
and ebbing, on a boulder by the entrance
when the moon is pale and distant, on a
certain annual midnight, sits a man with
artist's sketchbook, sits and gazes at the
harbor, dabbing with his sable brushes, when
the footsteps of a woman break the silence
of the darkness, cross the rocky promontory
to the painter with his sketchbook,

and she dances round his painting, plies the
brushes on the painting, and at last the man
and woman, barely showing in the
moonlight, meld together on the boulder,
and the midnight fills with laughter.

TO MY PREDECESSOR, ONCE REMOVED

—So many stories—

We share this same woman between us, the one
who sailed a canvas down the street in Hell's Kitchen,
long legs below, until you rescued her. You,
Paul Henreid, who sat beside her at the League.
When she stumbled back from her shrink sessions,
you listened patiently to passionate recaps.

You were there smiling gently, stroking her arm.
The Listener. And when you spoke, your English
flavored intriguingly with the suave echoes
of Berlin, she heard the kindness, the great
well of love, the acceptance, and marvelled
that she had come so far from California.

As you drew, she painted, you faithfully exact,
she fretful with form, in love with color,
intoxicated with words. During those years
she exposed herself to your calm eyes as she
has done these recent years for me, hence we
have the fountain of her in common, you and I.

Behind you a wealthy German past shattered
by Nazis, your father shot before your eyes,
your escape miraculous. To her you brought

the flavor of a world she knew from films,
for here you were, a Charles Boyer come true,
a handsome, calm and debonair European.

She waves her hands, flooded with memories.
I fold my arms and lean against the wall
opposite as you embraced and quieted her,
her energies at rest, at peace, composed
until the smoldering flared forth again
and she, who had your presence, wanted *you*.

New York lay at your feet. You walked the halls
of fashion. She began to show. Talk of the Town
included you. You basted her into *beau monde*—
and then became a Bahai. The sheer madness
of it appeals to me. You'd built with her
the glitter and the gold—and lost the glamour.

You accomplished a child, became suburbanites,
left them alone by day and dreamed by night.
You didn't lose your job, the job lost you.
And slowly, slowly you were losing her. She
wilted in that Levittown designed for pygmies
while you became what you had dreamed of.

You hovered close to them until you saw
her grasp for safety with another man
and you could leave with honor. And you did,
to the Southwest, ostensibly to take
Baha'ullah to the Indians, but I suspect
you sought simplicity, and died for it.

And now I have within my room your art,
"El Cavallo Negro", "Window Rock",
"Balcony House", "Ghost Ranch", "Apache Lake",
drawn with great openness and honesty.
My eyes swallow the grand vistas of your West;
my hand reaches out for yours, and takes it.

One day I caught a spider in a cloth
and she cried out, "Oh good! Take it outside!
Free it! It's Ted!" And so I did. She knew
you who were incapable of harm would come
back as a modest thing, to watch my love
approvingly, for her whom you have haunted.

And now she talks her iris into a giant frame,
Do it here! Here and here! Behave yourselves!
riding the jagged crests of emotion, fiercely
demanding as she devours her world
beginning with herself. She teaches me
the candescent art of moments and of days.

So many stories . . .

MYRTLE BEACH

After the scores of miles
of Carolina wilderness and the
occasional tobacco field,
we hit the Atlantic. Jo says,
Hey, the sun should be setting over it!
(That California woman!)
But the sun is back somewhere
lost in scrub pines and
drying sheds,
making the sky pink and hot but
we've left all that behind
and ahead is the perfect ocean.

Myrtle Beach is one outright
phenomenon,
Las Vegas East, family style, with
no loose women, gambling or
wedding parlors allowed.
But plenty of Carnival!
Got two roller-coaster rides,
water chutes, merry-go-rounds,
dodgems, video arcades, and
more and fancier mini-golf deals
than I knew existed.

The gulls fly high here
and far and few.
Jo sweeps crackers and bread into her purse
at The Captain's Table and

Tony's Italian
and throws scraps hopefully into the air
but no birds come.
The tourists are thick on the beach
and in the miles of motels.
Up and down the endless surf
their bright umbrellas march
in tidy rows.

It is holiday time, a good time
when we arrive at Myrtle Beach
and here is the fish-eyed lady
who runs the Inn
and sees these people who stare at sunsets.
She thinks Oh God two more
after thirty years of this.

They'll tramp sand into a room,
dirty sheets,
stop up the shower drain,
smear lipstick on towels,
and ask, Where's there a good place to eat around here?
But we don't do that, fish-eyed lady;
all we want is a tan,
and sand,
and sea,
and a smile from you.

We see the strand every hour,
and it comes to evening.
We nod at the honky-tonk town
with the streets aglitter
and the hot air thick with voices.
Oh there's fun everywhere, and
only the very young cry in the evening

over a cut or a dropped cone.
Otherwise tears are for later,
for motel rooms,
for cuts given voice,
for cruelties.
          Except for us.
We are full of affection
and easy laughter
even for the fish-eyed lady.

WOMAN BLEST

I drank tea with fanatics in Lahore.
In Isfahan I once disarmed a man
in fury at a Princess. There is more:
storms survived, sagas lived. American
diplomacy is hazardous to your health.
And with the years the game seemed somehow lost,
inane. As pointless as a poker bluff
in play with strangers. But the afflicted past
fades. She happened. Light came. I looked within
her and she me, and suddenly I could play host
to heroics because there was a heroine.
I am a different person, woman blest.
Perhaps the man intended. Days are sweet
and long. We lovers live where fables meet.

CONSPIRACY
WITH YELLOW ROSES

The power to dream: to live with her
and let ourselves grow old madly,
rush upon days and not let pain deter

or losses crush us out of a hot life.
Paint and write and let our hearts stir
at the edge of the dark. I want this wife

with hair flaming red over the gray,
eyes dancing, brush on fire like a knife
until canvas sings and her viewers may

tremble, uncertain what is this power,
like joy, like fierce sunlight, like day.
I want us to savor this hour

and ask any heaven or god not to scold
but leave us alone. Let our hunger devour
the good light. Let our bodies seem old

while we remain young. Not to live sadly
but with our nerves singing, to hold
fast to our flowers, and then to go gladly.

WITH TWENTY SEVEN THINGS TO SAY

A letter asks if I will go
and lecture, and I have a call
(I have too much time after all)
to publicize a coming show.

While White Oak mountain turns to mauve
I glue our red hearts to the glass,
look past them as the minutes pass,
not certain what I'm thinking of.

That Tryon ridges grow more tame?
That I make gestures to appear
more unconventional and queer
than once I was, and stay the same?

It's true, as day leads into night,
that I prefer Here more than There,
a house that sits precisely square,
with silvered cedar in the light,

my mate to love, my Sunday Times,
my current magazines, my checks,
the reassurance of our sex,
the tone of old ceramic chimes,

the way our eaves are deep and dark,

the privacy within our cave,
no voice to tell us to behave,
no critical Ecclese' arch.

But in this mood, I pause and call
with searching questions to a friend:
is this the end, the end, the end?
And is there nothing else at all?

Then like the bursting of the day
she rushes in with shining eyes,
amalgam of the fey and wise,
with twenty-seven things to say.

She lifts my heart. She takes me in.
Her joy surrounds me like the air.
In our own kingdom bright and fair,
we laugh and watch the world begin.

LONG-LEGGED LADY

Ah you with the long and tapered silken legs
that still me sleek and swollen well within
and do the dance for me, how comfort begs
me turn my back on you. But I begin

to understand—your love is yes for me
but more for self. How else can I explain
the inexplicable dichotomy
wherein the half of me remembers pain

but the sunlit side reflects your confidence.
We are a most unlikely wedded pair,
the sharp uncertainties, uneven eloquence,
the tortured doubts, the lives in disrepair

that somehow blossom, somehow flush with ache,
one for the other, and for the other's sake.

TO LOVE IN CALIFORNIA

How strange it is to think of you
three hours apart from me
this very moment. Is it true
that time has changed? To be

or not to be must now be seen
not as Shakespearean rhyme
but as a quandry caught between
Eastern and Pacific Time.

Surely my remote mandrake
will lose none of its power?
Time has no charge to make
a difference by the hour.

But if I sprouted wings to fly
five hours to profit three,
you could be out of town-and I
would be alone with me.

No cock can crow across the land,
no chick can recompense
for what is sadly out of hand
with three hours' difference.

So how much better if we come
together in this bed,
with Time in equilibrium
and Rose inspirited.

EXODUS

We gather up our things around this place,
fold the carpets from my Persian past,
sell silver from an old passion,
donate clothes out of fashion,
do the things one must do at the last
when it's time to look into the other's face

and ask, shall we keep this souvenir?
that lovely copper tray from Isfahan?
this box of old letters?
Or do we throw off fetters
and test what it is we're truly set upon
such as good books and a small beer?

We laugh a lot while sorting out the store
of tarnished jewelry and old ties,
read to each other diaries
and give and take inquiries,
knowing we have no need for lies,
no call for pretty poses any more.

We pack what is to keep: a Pushtoon knife
as sharp as sin, her painting of a chair,
a sofa-bed for sleeping.
We are what we are keeping:
the will to paint and write. To be aware
of death, not more. To spend our lives on life.

THE MOVE

We are giving up our things.
We are toying with brave ideas
such as living lightheartedly
without material dependencies.

It is such a small decision
that we are surprised by it when
it rams through like a wild wind
scouring, insisting, coming again

and leaves us drained and stunned,
butterflies out of a cocoon, sticky,
fluttering uncertainly into the sun
and surprised at our own beauty.

We look for food enough,
and warmth, and always somewhere for flowers
and a dark dry nest for resting
and a hungry life measured in hours.

ATLANTIS

But why does the water stop at the shore?,
she asks, and I have no answer for her.
Yes, of course, I do speak of gravity, how there
must be a down settling of things, no more.
Oh I've heard all that, she cries, but how could
anything stop that water which flows like blood?

It is the blood of earth, I say. It is worn
over the skin, and all of the skin is land.
Oh but it will wash up here, she cries. Nothing can
stop it! It will tumble us around! We will be torn
apart and it will fling us every which way!
But it hasn't since the rough first sun, I say,

and therefore I think it won't do so now.
You are such an optimist, she says, and stares
expectantly out. What else can I tell her? Where's
the flood? We have been here forever. How
can she fear the unchanging?

We will now dine
at our glass table on rich food and splendid wine.

A SOFTING WISDOM

Again the course of words leads me along
to place a sacrifice before your feet,
making a hesitation of my song
because I feel a failure of conceit

to find the tribute that best honors you,
my darling lady. If I may proclaim
a softing wisdom and a hard virtue
to build a glad caprice around your name,

it would be thus: that you have seen in me
not common goodness but a buried lust
for that which promises to set me free.
Since simple justice is not always just,

I form the awkward measure of a man
from what you will, and what I will, and can.

THE IMPRESARIOS

No one will know we make our way to bed
to sculpt the pillows and lie back and look
beyond the other's eyes, inhabited.
No one will sense your drama or my book

of dreams. We lie in darkness, woman, man,
birthing vignettes. No one will ever guess
how you become a fabled artisan,
while I observe a passionate caress

in Isfahan. No one would ever find one
half the wild adventures that we face,
that ricochet within your sleeping mind
or mine, adjacent in this common space.

Each is a practiced impresario
behind night's curtain—but no one will know.

LOVE IS YOUR ART

Among the thousands of words I weave and write
to touch our time as it goes ticking by,
I caress these several as favorite
because of you, because you magnify

the simple rhythm of a thought. My art
is amplified by reason of loving you,
and yet affection flourishes in part
since you include me with a retinue

of others. Even while loving, for my sake
I give you space. I know you with the rest.
I keep myself, observant while you speak
to proxy daughters, surrogate for the best

of mother, sister, friend. Love is your art
and I must lift you lightly to my heart.

THE PAINTER

I stood behind her, above
her shoulder, to watch her trace
colors on canvas. My love
warmed me and her red hair
flamed the sea. "Negative space!"
she cried. "It's the *where!*
But how can I paint the *gull?*
How can I watch it move
and pretend that it's frozen there?"

My heart heaved
and trembled. I have grieved
for artists ever since.
The fire and innocence
which are a painter's norm
could see a gull as it appears
cleaving the sky,
study it savagely with tears
but only define its form,
unable to make it fly.

Is her heart full?
Is that why she's still there,
in battle with empty air?
When my negative space
is all but her face?

VICTOR NOIR

We saw the effigy of Victor Noir
in Paris in the *Cimetiere du Pere La Chaise,*
as though he'd fallen in bronze, his face
angelic, and we asked around for
the reason he lay there dead
at twenty-five, splendidly dressed,
his top hat ready, as if he'd digressed
enroute to the Opera. They said

(entre nous) he was envied by most
of the dandies of Paris—he fell
in a duel after loving too well.
For a great gift a great cost.
Now he lay at our feet. Childless young
women for the past hundred years
had rubbed his cod shiny (the dears
worshipped where he was well hung).

My lady slanted her eyes at me
and I looked decorously down.
A siren trumpeted in the town,
a fresh breeze stirred and we
photographed where Victor lay
victoriously on his shelf,
supremely, shamelessly himself,
and turned and went our way.

TO WATCH HER DANCE WITH FLOWERS

In a far country, a diplomat set free
out of the lapis-lazuli of my past,
a last walk out of a last Embassy,
knowing only that life was Janus-faced,

that only the lapis-lazuli was mine,
and one day then to sit on a rock and meet
a woman, and be reminded that love is blind,
that it selects, not you, that life is sweet,

that there's no sentence from the past.
Her eyes know colors like virtues, virtues like the rainbow.
Paletted in pain, her canvasses sing with skies,
and seas and rocks invade her studio.

While I stand by to watch her dance with flowers
she kisses the minutes and forgets the hours.

HER SONG TO THE GULLS BELOW GUN CLIFF

Lustrous and silent the wings
but harsh and croaking the cries
of your shrill gull bickerings.
With cold cutting killer's eyes
and beaks blade-bent like a kris
you tear at the bowels of fish.

Bribed by an offering of bread
you plummet in on one crust
among many, but scream there instead
of sharing. Gulls are not just.
As selfish as children at play
you bicker an Eden away.

But I lure you here to my side,
cocking your shark's head,
simple and pure in your greed,
demanding of me to be fed.
I may flinch at your icy stare
but I marvel at you in the air.

We have a thing for each other,
thoroughly understood:
I am your earthbound mother
as long as I bring you food;
while for me your white wings leaven

the space between sea and heaven.

Bring your bird-children to me
to float above my red hair;
your monstrous manners make free
of those of us who would care-
but I can forgive you such things,
you sailors on silver wings.

LIKE YOU

The iris are happy and brightly exotic, like you—
saucy and secret and deeply erotic, like you—
They thrive near the shores of this village aquatic,
and they throw me into conditions hypnotic,
narcotic, quixotic, a trifle neurotic
when I swallow your love like a petal osmotic.
Thankfully you're not even slightly despotic!
My caution goes flying in feelings chaotic
on glimpsing delights 'neath your trousers culottic-
so I sing you my love in words semiotic
that suit the beaut of a woman pyrotic, like you—

0 wow . . .

THE FILM LOVER

The little man with the bright button eyes
in a kind face gestured. "When I see her
I go all puddly." We stood outside his cinema
and watched your long legs striding up Broad Street
in the early evening. And the red hair.

> First the Volunteer. "You lot,"
> said the Publican's wife, "You'll see anything."
> What was playing? All I remember
> is that your red hair flamed
> over the seatback when I returned
> with the Whippies and gave you yours.
> I read gratitude in your wide expectant eyes
> that flicked back to the blank screen,
> already captured, waiting for Pearl and Dean.

Waiting . . . watching . . . charmed
by the Intermission's small bandy-legged
woman marching up and down the aisles
selling from her tray of goodies.

> You woman child of Hollywood
> who keeps trying to go home.

But can't. New York owns part of you,
other pages of your diary own part of you.
Maine and Dorset and Surrey own part of you.

I own part of you.

And you own all of it. Of us.
Of me. Of the little man with his
    bright button eyes.

THE ARTIST IN AN ACT OF KINDNESS

Between the stone rows, the vanities
of those remaining for those gone,
the artist searched for a certain tomb,
the modest plot of Modigliani's.

He who had been careless about living
lay weedy with neglect. Upon his grave
flowers had died old. The coarse grass gave
a coarse feel, as if by not surviving

he had given up his need for caring.
She who came knelt by his stone,
picked off the dead leaves one by one,
pulled up the grasses, carefully clearing

the chiselled Amadeo, sleeping
with his Jeanne [1]. She went to claim
fresh red roses reflective of his fame
and fixed them and sat silent, weeping.

---

[1] Jeanne Hebuterne lived with Amadeo Modigliani from 1917 to his death in
1920, killed herself when he died and is buried beside him in Paris's *Cimetere
du Pere La Chaise*.

THE AMERICAN LADY

Now the tall Richard walks the streets
and cries his cry. He wears the black tricorn
handsomely over his bearded face and his horn
of a voice echoes between the shops. He meets
a cluster of tourists and starts on a round
of Cobb Gate and Buddle Bridge, the Guild-
hall and, he tells them, here is Gun Cliff
where the American lady may be found

feeding her gulls. Richard leans over
and the tourists crowd the broad ledge
beside him, craning for a view which
is her on a stone platform. The river
pours out below her right arm and flows
to sea over rumpled rocks. Her auburn hair
shows recklessly against Gun Cliff where
years have gentled the edges. A gull flies

past her from the Lym's canyon of stone
and flares up over dozens more. Further out
is the rippled Bay under one enormous cloud.
The tourists can see for miles. They rest upon
the ledge. Their voices are like a sigh
sifted from noisy cities. They look through
cameras, snapping the Cobb, the sweeping view,
and one or two the American who happily

scatters bread to the birds, oblivious
of Richard and the group. She makes a small
disturbing scene—by stone and wall
poised for the Holidays, with omnivorous
focussed gulls demanding to be fed,
and the watchers, the feeder with her mind
empty and open, willing to send
floating on Lym water the nourishing bread.

ONE DAY AND ONE NIGHT

Lyme Regis, 1984
An American Chronicle

To go flying around the earth
and to end up here, that is my own
felt miracle. To make a birth
with her at this stage, in this town,
that is another. I will herein
spell the small shapes of it, the bright
form of now, the phenomenon
of a cycle, one day and one night.

While she sets up the television,
or the telly as they call it here,
I labor over another revision
("You'd like this Humphrey Bogart, dear-")
of some troubling lines. I can't say
I don't watch the telly. I really do
("I taped 'The Way We Were' today!")
but we have fifteen films to view

and at the moment I must go
fishing in this old fishing town
for meat wherewith to cook a stew,
lettuce for salad making, brown
rice, a pint of milk, some figs,

the TIMES, some chocolate, some gin,
and back to our uncommon digs
and where the record must begin.

The flat spreads spaciously for two:
entry, bedrooms, living, den,
kitchenette and baths. We knew
on arrival that the space had been
waiting for us. Our eyes can reach
out from the battlement of our room
to the safety of a compact beach
and the Cobb (which for now will subsume

congeries of boats and the Sailing Club
by its great breakwater's curve)
and to the bulk of the Cobb Arms Pub
across our street. We can observe
all the circumstances—holiday shops
on the circle, shuttered icecream stands,
crowded in summer when a legion troops
through hourly, and now when winter lends

the place a hooded dignity,
an occasional echoing car going through
and the FRESH FISH van scooting busily
toward the Sailing Club where the last few
fishing boats offload. But otherwise
it is quiet. Only the sea performs.
We are listeners to soliloquies
of salt water. Winter reaffirms

the eloquence of sea. Lyme Bay
can gentle itself for visitors
but with the weakness of pale day
in this land of long nights it stirs

darkly. We feel we are in a fort,
a haven, almost primevally safe
against the storms. The ancient port
protects us and within our fief

the walls are two feet thick, of stone
quarried two hundred years ago
to build a warehouse. It has known
trade goods from many a land. Below
were stacked the rolls of sober cloth
that ended up as Wessex wear,
the barrelled tea trundled by wroth
porters, spices, farming gear,

brandy, coarse tobacco, silk
(such goods that were not sunk by weights
offshore, to wait for those who skulk
past midnight). Massive wooden gates
between the Fish Shop and the Marine
Antiquarian Books open into
a courtyard. Now my heroine
stands on our outside stairs (we do

without an inside route) to greet
me after I've returned the car
into our slot. It's her conceit
to cock a hip. her scimitar
arms behind her massed red hair,
and do a bump and grind. I drop
my produce bag (hooked by a snare
far older than I am), do not stop

to collect a thing. I shout and chase
her up the wrought-iron stairs and catch
her on our bed—within the space
of a minute, from shopping to White Witch.

I hold her close, my sorceress,
sated, to look at "Winter in Lyme",
lavender against a wall of white, the thrust
of "Bird in Flight" nearby, and grim

on the space above our bed, "The Sheep".
Elsewhere in the room seascapes glow
and storms rage, demanding from me a deep
involvement. Her pulse and moods I know
as I know my own: the cocky, the sure,
the vulnerable. She forges good
from the cruel years of being poor,
mixing her beauty with her blood.

"I'm *an artist!*" she cries. "But how can I
ever paint again? Do you see those rocks?
My paintings always mystify
me!" (Her passion overlooks
enormous skill. She uses love
to conjure confidence and fights
her art until she wins.) We move
hallwards, congenial opposites,

and I leave her for the tiny room
I write in, a garden for my mind,
my study, carelessly stolen from
the main salon. Here I am blind
and see more and more. A desk,
two chairs, typewriter, shelves of books,
a potted fern, a battered chest
filled with junk. Everything looks

lived in, lived on (what I have left
of the days of my life). My four
children, graphically enfiefed
(though one is gone). The exterior

of the Universe. The splendid TIMES
Atlas of the World. Her two,
her pride. And scattered magazines.
A Khattack plain tree leaf daubed blue

from my friend Khush. Original oils
by my love, some trees, an earthy nude,
a seascape (lashing water boils
against some rocks), a flower of rude
crude passion, a curious lion's head,
a profiled boy. Among prints
by masters famous and long dead.
In this small room I have an intense

exposure to her and her few friends-
such as Da Vinci, Picasso, and on the sill,
a fine Modigliani nude which blends
with the rest. (Here one can tell
that beauty is left love.) I return
to the big room where she's enchaired
and enchanted. I quickly learn:
that the fishermen today have fared

quite well—gulls swirl above their boats
like bright confetti; Golden Cap
is non-pareil, its pinnacle glows
in a rare late sun; she is enrapt
by a windsurfer whose whipping sail
catches the light; she holds the scene
of evening tightly, the fading pale
soft English coastal dusk. I mean

she has been captured by this place;
she stares at the sea as if she would
write on its pulsive waves. Her face
is quick and mobile with the mood

of a wondering child's. She has tasted
quiet here but stays tremendously
excited. Lyme should have been
wasted on her, and it's an odd anomaly

that one who is New York and L.A.
should fall in love with Dorsetshire
and live six thousand miles away
from her past, and be quite unaware
of inconsistency. My story
is a recital of the opposite,
begun in a kind of allegory
of Arcadia, a requisite

innocence that led through strange
deflowerings into the hectic life
of a diplomat; a sea change
with a new Carolina wife,
with endless energy, a sense
of destiny, enough ambition
and a thirst for the odd experience.
That, with a pleasant disposition,

has brought me to this different scene.
This one comes near and puts her arms
around my chest. "Somebody's been
thinking." "But thinking never harms
anybody." "You it does, my love.
You go back to the sad years."
"Ah, yes." I shall have to remove
myself from that. Or try. My fears

flail away against dangers of other
times. When has she ever said
something cruel? That was the other
wife long ago, and she is now dead.

I am with this one, and this I know,
as a late sun kisses her cheek and embosses
her red hair, I can no longer go
to a daughter gone. Listing my losses

is closing the window on the sun
to sit in a darkened cell. Not much
sense in that. What's done is done.
I unwrap a hand and gently touch
her cheek. The rest of the living room
is an odd mixture of the really good:
her lively oils, an amaryllis bloom,
a potted ivy, a sandalwood

and ivory Bombay girl, the rug
I inherited from Khan Yahya Khan
(back when my strange travelogue
of a life centered in Isfahan),
a fine old sculpted table-stall,
an elegant ill-treated trunk
of some pale wood. That's about all.
The space might be shabby and poor, I think,

but my artist's sharp and splendid
eye makes it a whole. Here we've a chance
(to put the point instructively)
to participate in Shiva's dance,
to balance on this particular time
our pasts and futures. In this now
(in a converted warehouse flat in Lyme),
together, to discover how,

for us, two fey expatriates,
in circumstances now and then
precarious, how, when the fates
contrive to be signally mean,

how, by fleeing from our brood,
by joining up in a fugitive
autonomy (believing we could
in this environ), how to live.

The night here seems like any night
'til breached by the fitful sound of sea.
The ocean dark relentlessly
swallows the frivolity of light,
maintains a certain pace and roll,
moves in endlessly with the kiss
of slithering shingle, signalling us
with a fantastic chronicle,

a tale of rhythm without rhyme,
of constant form, of negative space
told in a whisper in this place,
this final destination, Lyme.
But a rocket goes up. She and I
look at each other over our stew
a breathless moment, then comes two,
exploding somewhere in a sky

made palpable by sound, but dark
as a witch's hat. We hurry and stand
by a window (comfortably on land)
as the Lifeboat crew and boat embark.
Men have always challenged the sea
(a living thing beyond control).
We watch the lights of the Lifeboat roll
and disappear. Men tend to be

arrogant and stubbornly blind to life,
and even more to death
until, between a breath and a breath,
the sea will suddenly remind

them of their fragile state. We dress
and go to walk along the Cobb.
Summer would see a curious mob
but now a pervasive emptiness

hovers static over the port
and the wind has risen. Somewhere out
on the hidden water, somewhere about,
are the crew of volunteers and the boat
and someone in trouble. I am aware
of the island this is, a floating land
carefully, tortuously defined
and left by time in disrepair,

a cocky isolate that has known
an empire, these days grown small,
peripheral and skeptical,
faded from history too soon
for many of us. The men have returned
from Charmouth in their rubber barque
by pounding through tumultuous dark,
the mission fruitless; they've just learned

the screams a caller claimed he heard
below Black Ven out from the beach
(where high tides occasionally overreach
the unwary) may have been a bird.
Resigned, they drive away. We stroll
back to Marine Parade. The din,
as white foam bands come curling in
and shingle beats its tambour roll,

strikes echoes off pink cottages lit
by amber streetlamps. Picturesque.
She presses my hand. I pause and ask,
"Is this beautiful? Or sad? Isn't it
possible men might, someday, somehow

wreck-?" She says, "You think too much!
We're here, now!" I'm caught by such
emotion I'm not certain how

to answer. She takes my hand. We go
to the nearby shadowed railing where
I watch her grip the bar and stare
into the violence down below—
"You! Sea!" she cries. "I'm *painting* you!
What are you doing?" (In my head
is a vision of a huge helmeted
astonished Neptune.) It is true

the cottages' pale modest pink
won't last, but is my artist right-
what is important is this sight
this moment of this surf? I think
too much. How is this moment mine?
Well . . . it's miracle enough, to be
in Lyme beside a restless sea,
with her, along The Walk, at nine

on a Saturday evening. Maybe I've done
a Prodigal Son who has returned
to find that absence hasn't earned
him entry. But she's as American
as I am-and somehow she knows
that it doesn't matter. We are here
for an indefinite sabbatical year.
I think too much. Sometimes it shows.

My definition of a strength
could be a weakness. Thinking stops
me halfway through a door. Eve adapts
and strides through. No arm's length.
No fear. Ah, well. The Volunteer

greets us with laughter. Our outer coats
come off. Under the chamber pots
that bedeck the ceiling, we guzzle a beer

and smile through the smoky haze at our host,
our genial giant, a gentle face
with a pirate's beard. There's hardly space
to stand. Our faithful pianist,
Nellie, takes one hand from the keys
and squeezes ours. She starts to play
'*The Yanks are coming!*" *and* a gray-
haired baritone shouts, "Nellie, *please!*

They're already *here*'" After the laugh
we sing and it sounds still more like home,
old clan festivities, and some
we know, maybe half, but the other half
seems familiar, as if we'd lived
this once, these "Voli" sing-alongs,
the tinkling piano, the old songs.
From exile, we long to be retrieved

by Englishness. I realize
then, that the Bass is a strongish beer
which maketh a lovely haze, my dear,
through which to sing and fraternize.
We go to the bar where Marilyn says,
"Next week you two will want to go
to the Guildhall chambers for the show.
There's a mare matin'. Indeed, it is

the grandest event of the year!" I look
at my love as she turns to me . . .
in both our fertile minds we see
Shires at the Guildhall door; a book
with blood line records out of which

stud deals are made. "But how in hell,"
I ask, "can mares climb that stairwell?"
And then, it is as if a switch

turns off all sound. "Well-you know-
you said 'mare matin"-" "Oh my lord!"
our hostess cries. "You lot! My word
was 'Mayor'. 'May-yore!"' She bestows
her most withering look. "Mayor *meeting!*"
Silence erupts into general glee,
the roar of laughter envelopes me
and mine, and then our host is treating

us to another round. Our speech
has the shape of a different land
and I lead a Shire horse with my hand
up the spiral Guildhall stairs. They teach
us with laughter. I say goodbye
with wary affection. Our embrace
brings a smile to Nellie's gentle face
and we leave the Pub. The nimble sky

has shed the storm. A flock of clouds
is scurrying by like Dorset sheep
with the full moon shepherding. A deep
gunmetal heaven. She applauds.
"Where else in the world could we find that Pub?"
"Well-not in Isfahan," I say,
"but maybe in downtown LA.?"
"Oh *you!*" she cries. "Or find the Cobb?"

I interrupt: "Or drink such beer?
I take my hat off to that Bass!
Do you think I made a proper ass
of myself'!" "For sure!" she says. "A year
from now, or even five years hence,

they'll tell about this Yankee pair
and horses on the Guildhall stair!"
She chokes with laughter. Our romance

has the two of us as its flesh. It thrives
on our painting and writing (she asserts
that the thing about painting is, it hurts)
(the thing about writing is, it lives
on digested episodes of pain).
Somehow our laughing makes us whole.
I take her hand. We turn and stroll into
Langmore Gardens. Once again

I think about language. We are here,
Americans, as visitors
but also as inheritors.
This speech is easy on the ear
because it is ancestral. My
memory knows it. If I try
I can't speak other than what I
learned from them. What potency

it gives them over us. A Club
we have no option but to join,
where membership defines our coin.
We feel at ease beside the Cobb
because adventurers from here
were filled with greed and ignorance,
because they took a mortal chance,
too stubborn to buckle in to fear,

and sailed for lands too cold for Spain.
We're here as visitors, and yet
they are our history, our debt
and asset. Modern Englishmen
touch us with ties that outlast steel:
our past, our tongue. Forgotten Kings

acculturated us with strings
attached. And when we think or feel

we do so in their language. Well,
enough of that. I think too much.
The point is this, all tongues are rich
or poor if we make them so. We tell
ourselves. And furthermore, I move
(her hands are warm and talkative)
that any dialect could give
me songs to celebrate my love.

*   *   *

It's morning. Isfahan has used
the rising sun and sent it on.
I check the Bay, the Cobb, bemused
and curious. This much abused
phenomenon called life is fun.
At least today. At least for one.
I look at her red rumpled hair
and quietly ease out of there

and dress in jogging togs and go
down to Marine Parade. My hands
grip kilo weights. I try to throw
arms high and swing them to and fro
naturally. Power walking demands
an effort my body understands
and seems prepared to give. The sea
speaks hidden tongues, only to me.

All right. The world needs fixing. I'm
trying to think how. Let's imagine that
we accept wholeness as a paradigm.
I'm talking about the antonym
of reductionism. Let's create

world-wide agreement—a postulate
that parts are secondary to the whole
(let the bugles blare! Let the drums roll!)

and the Chinese leadership must agree
to step aside, the Russians pledge
democracy, the Haitians free
elections, and naturally we
will ourselves accept the tutelage
of the United Nations (I average
about twenty minutes for my walk
which gives me time enough to talk

the average King into common sense).
With the world set right I go upstairs
and shave and shower. The evidence
is that the job is too immense
so I think I'll have breakfast. Tea prepares
a body for anything: England fares
forth to empire, the Chinese
to incredible lasting dynasties.

I'm still at table, still with tea,
when I hear a cry from the cozy bed.
It's my love's waking call for me.
She's come to day expectantly
as drama fades inside her head.
I join her with deliberate speed
to catch the tendrils of the dream,
the cast, the plot, the Freudian theme.

For fifteen minutes by her side,
smiling at her excited face,
I share theatre with my bride,
her skills as raconteur deployed
for an audience of one. The space

of her dreaming time is large, profuse
with possibilities (she comes
with phantasmagoric premiums).

We walk on the Cobb's massive wall
to the further end where Meryl Streep
once stood in her unconventional
part in the town's exceptional
experience with film. The steep
climb where Smithson took the step
that changed his life. Here is the French
Lieutenant's Woman—my posturing wench

for a moment plays in the starring role,
her eyes cast back at me, and I
step up as Charles and venture all
and rescue her, a curious gull
as onlooker, an apricot sky
as scrim. To be or not to be
is never a question for her; she *is*.
She's proof of her own hypothesis

that I'm still trying to define:
that life is joy? (Which sounds too kitch.)
A feast? (Where she's ordained to dine,
the table spread with food and wine).
I suppose it doesn't matter much—
the end phenomenon is such
a wonder, on this fragile point
of time and space and temperament.

Magnificent colors! Radiant dyes!
That's how I visualize her world.
She throws cerulean into skies,

paints orange rocks and rhapsodies
of tumbled water. I have quarreled
with symmetries while she has curled
lopsided horns on the brilliant sheep
that snorts above us while we sleep.

She tells me that I'm Capricorn.
That would postulate my days
are different since I was born
on an icy January night. I earn
my life-but the subtle ways
I sift through opportunities
are locked into Uranus and Mars
and my answers lie among the stars.

Well . . . that may be. The flow and flux
of living with her might come about
from stars. She's not what one expects
in a housemate of the opposite sex.
But nerve and free will get my vote.
We make ourselves. (A fishing boat
moves out. Gulls scream. The sounds of town
drift across to us.) In a baritone,

I say to Meryl Streep, "My dear,
a lovely morning. May I inquire-
were you considering settling here?
Marvelous people. Splendid beer."
"It's not the public I desire,"
she cries, "it's *you!* What I require
is a Capricorn who has your face!"
With that I publicly embrace

her, and we turn toward town and bow.
And we look at each other. Morning has
cleared the air. We have moved through
from light to dark to light. Here's how
a cycle has ended, the day that was
and the night, the whirl of yesterdays
spinning toward tomorrows: she and I
and the Cobb and the town and the apricot sky.

SHARING A MAINE AUTUMN

We find a way through blueberries after a
picnic on a far hill, to stand silently, watching
the painted leaves, the sky paling over a
valley with its open arms.

We stroll now down the slope without a cloud,
nothing but warmth from a Maine sun shining.
We walk slowly, still green grass bedding our feet,

and your joy in each blade is infectious,
and my joy in your joy is enduring.
We skirt pines and bright birches. We find warm stones

to sit on, mountains to see, talking to do,
and the sweet bounty of blueberries. We
touch ripe leaves falling, fading flowers, an
old tumbled wall. Our hands

when we are eldering will have known this
tendering, this stream where we link arms,
laugh easily and have no tears. The ripening

that is not an ending. The stream that will flow on forever.

THIS WEEK
SHE HAS PAINTED

her story on stone, the artist: a huge rock
that thrusts itself sullen above sea, as timeless
as bone with the crustings of age, a shell
for decoration, a wild wig of weeds, wrack
and kelp, tangle and reeds, a rich pattern
of pebbles thrown as offerings, clamshells in their beds.

Old treasure lies moldering here under green
lichen and, yes, it is all sea but a rock that
a privateer would remember. She has fingered
in Braille a mountain behind it, lifting from shore
with forests of pines, its superior heights humbled
by clouds that appear tumbled and gray,
making ready for more.

She paints the tangle, the maelstrom of stalks,
rockweed and algae, the surging of brine over
lazuli pebbles, a water that talks the language
of corsairs bold as the line of color she daubs,
her palette spun-golding ocean and rock, as if treasure
is molding some depth of her thought, with her brush
and its strokes and the rock and the sea and her eyes
         hundredfolding.

THIS WOMAN

This woman holds the stick brush in her hand,
baton to conduct a counterpoint in color.

She mixes her paints until there is summoned
from strange writhing ocher earths, from some

chamber ten levels down, out of earthy growth
into her mind, swelling out of her artist eyes

and flowing out of her brushes, a fecundity
as if of wombs and breasts, resolved to spill

its fertile spores onto the blank invitation
of canvas. It is pain made joy. Sometimes too much,

so that she must dance or sing or fall exhausted
into a chair. But working, it is as though

the sea writhing its fat storms around the earth
and the land spouting its rules about restraint

mean nothing. She laughs and defies my firm logic
like a flower pushing the dull inhibiting ground,

determined amid the doubts of night to be a rose.

SUCH BEADS OF TIME

I hide inside with you without a light,
caress your flesh that well remembers pain
and guard you from the snow this frigid night,
the raucous world, the pressing sounds of men.

Your voice recalls our yesterdays. I touch
your once and lovely soft sleeked artist's hands
as if in unbelief. For see, the much
of too far few tomorrows comes and strands

us here, exiles in temporality,
to finger out our days, such beads of time
to count as gifts. But I've the luxury
of unripe youth's productive antonym-

to see, and know, and smile, and not to care
as long as I can love, and you are here.

LIKE A CAUGHT GHOST

my shadow stills
when the rose moment beds beneath
your eyes. Your slow smile teases
like October after summer sleep.

Shall we loop chains of paper thoughts
to touch the night, the autumn moon?

You girl me with that wealth of hair
until it aches behind my blood

and summer's tastes are ripening
to love in an October wood.

KIND HEARTS

So much has happened to me in these years.
Too much to recollect, but not enough
to satisfy my debt. I'm in arrears
to love. I played a game of blindman's-buff

before I touched the other in the dark
and knew that face, and knew that special skin.
She came with me and warmed a frozen heart,
taught me to see, a joyous heroine

who showed explosive colors through her eyes,
brought me to smell the roses, held my hand
through pain, read over what I wrote with wise
partiality—and helped me understand

a miracle: only kind hearts can prove
the everlasting youthfulness of love.

I DO FORGET

I do forget, and then because I must
confess, I come back home without the thing
I went for, and she laughs and says, My King,
it's only that you are a genius.

And so I take her in my arms, absolved
and instantly absurdly lightened of
the dull and tedious. Within her love
a warm propitious climate has evolved

and it shall storm no more, and I will be
inebriate of flesh and mouth and eyes,
a proselyte of freshness and surprise,
no longer mortified by memory.

It is as if, for me, she opens wide
the doors to mansions that I have foregone
for dry success, for hollow victories won.
In rich profusion when we go inside

are all the roses of her life, the blooms
of yesterdays, of flowers unknown to me,
vase after vase, as far as love can see.
Her mansion holds a multitude of rooms.

HOMECOMING

Don't frighten me again with silence.
Write me your every breath; I want
you here. With me. Your plane taxies
across tarmac, obedient ship.
I wait as a stewardess leads you,
returned from a long yesterday,
pale and leaning. Ah my bird.

> Fragile, fluttering the neutral air,
> my Cardinal with a torn wing,
> and all I can give are these arms
> as awkward as old branches,
> or this rough shoulder like
> a gnarled embracing maple
> smelling of autumn and love.

Look up, lady. You warm my heart
trying so hard to stand, smiling
as if absence had never been.
You make muffled morning sounds
like a bedroom tousled with sleep.
When I look at you I tremble
at your realness. Ah my bird.

HER PASSIONATE AND CARELESS WAYS

She paints, and makes an ordinary day
transform to brilliant color while I stalk
some dank elusive verb that slips away.
And then I hear her laugh and come awake

to what a gift she is. This lady has
the power to fire my words and make me come
back to her passionate and careless ways
as to a Scorpio's curriculum.

She lifts my heart. I wonder how she knows
such texts of tenderness, the word, the kiss
that heals a hidden wound. I think she chose
me with a gentleness, the antithesis

of what I'd known, and tends me for these years
as with a garden green from forgotten tears.

GIRLS AND BOYS TOGETHER

Bitter white the winter,
green and sweet the spring.
Beyond summer gardens
autumn's honeying.

Girls and boys together,
woman will and man,
storming through the always
before love has gone.

Men are like a language
someone heaves to her—
she must milk his meaning,
panting out her power.

Fast we moan the moment,
smooth we sing the sky,
delicate the dreaming,
wondering the why.

FOR JO IN OCTOBER

She waltzes like an abstract
painting across the rug,
swinging her hips into
the mellow orange of maples,
      her shoulders into brown
      branches, her moccasins down
      at the end of long legs
      into the color of a Maine
          autumn. And ablaze
          with color are her cheeks,
          and the fire in her eyes.

Her mobile face makes
a romance of the time
that brought her here into my
waiting arms with
      her humor, a laughing
      into the restless wind.
      Like October leaves red
      with their triumphant
          recession from life,
          she draws her passion
          from the astonishing years.

THE GARLIC PAINTING

A giant garlic clove
on a high cliff above
surging waters is my lissome
love's bottom, her well rounded bum,
and the sea's patterns move
along her thighs, and waters come
eddying around a crevice
while I watch like a novice
in the old art of love,
an amateur in what she's mistress of.

Mistress of a subtle shade
in the swell of well made
breasts that she thinks of as skin
even while knowing that what lies within
is what I crave. And I have often said
this to her, and Josephine
smiles sweetly, that buxom Miss,
and by some metamorphosis
do I her garlic enfilade,
this Everywoman willing to be laid.

FEEL AS A WOMAN FEELS

What have you come to mean to me, attuned
to your name? That you survive with fire
behind caress. That when I touch your wound
you arch and sing me secret your desire,

swallow my strength and titillate my tongue,
and meld with me so full and primitive
that I would shed an arm to be as young
as such love calls for. Your provocative

and eagle's eyes are ancient harlotry
but you remain touchingly unaware,
softened in innocence. I would not be
flesh-drunk, lip-sotted but I deeply care

about your passion. Loving you, I can
feel as a woman feels, and stay a man.

THE PAINTED WOMAN

sits nude on a dark
triangular chair, and
looks thoughtfully out.
Sardonically? Or
faintly pleased with herself?
She hides herself behind
the pose.

One hand touches the seat
in a casual caressing gesture,
as poised as a ballerina.

The other hand
lies along her inner thigh
almost coyly, almost hiding
the delta.

Her hips form a warm ivory
carving against the hard
dark wood, the flesh
a double cream with a rich
hint of yellow.

Her long torso,
her full moon breasts,
push her into the room
smelling faintly of musk.

She whispers, the waiting woman,
so that only the artist can hear.
And she sits there, her skin, her face,
her body her own because
only the artist can share.

Oh Lady, move your eyes
to me.

VALENTINE'S DAY

Valentine's Day. The fast beat of our hearts,
our metronomes of love, opposing faces,
flesh unto flesh, and it all starts
with our vague gestures toward the Graces,

Aglaia and Thalia and Euphrosyne,
docked at a pier in Greece. Their craft
has come ashore, and will be mine
and yours, the two of us abaft,

holding our breath, pirates of pleasure,
hyperboles of love, speaking a tongue
secret with soft caress, a treasure
locked in our growing hearts since young,

and we shall sail this sea, the Graces here
as crew, and steer this ship, our home,
through calm or raging waters—without fear—
and Charon keep his vigil till we come.

ST. VALENTINE

They say roses are red and violets are blue,
and sending a Valentine means I love you.

But what's the true story of this special day?
It was named after Valentine who, so they say,

was Bishop of Terni, later martyred in Rome,
and who, when he went to his Heavenly home,

was somehow made into the symbol of love.
But what's to believe? What can we prove?

For others say No! The Saint was a priest
who, when Terni was slain, was already deceased.

But our sending of cards has no basis, in truth,
it's just an upsurge of emotions in youth,

and the date was selected (depending on what
your authority is) because the love-knot
coincided with Rome's Lupercalia Feast,
or perhaps it was when the songs never ceased

of the birds in the Spring—or that's what I hear,
but whatever the reason, we don't really care,

we will all smell the roses, and violets blue,
and burble sweet nothings about loving you!

COVENANT

My woman speaks nostalgically
of lively loves, of seldom sleeps,
of leaching lovers of desire.

Her stories live inside her,
ever changing, always fresh
for this new lover and new friend.

I place rose petals in her hair,
convey affection to her eyes.
She gives to the deep need

I have enhollowed in my heart,
content before her tender power
to barter flowers for her smile.

CONFESSION OF THE CLUMSY MAN

I love you. It's that simple, but as though
there's room for confusion, I still somehow
manage to step on your toe, or kiss you
          and kiss you and kiss you

until you can't breathe. Sometimes I forget
what it was that you wanted, or ask several
times what you've told me—and yet
          helping you is my favorite task,

my true labor of love. When I trip, it's from
trying to be graceful for you. But I seem an
apprentice in romance. Let my hands cup
          your face and I manage

to mess up your hair; where I mean to be
gentle, I find that I sound doctrinaire or the
thrust of my speech seems somehow unkind.
          My excuse is that I am in love.

You are my rose, my romance. If I stumble
while trying to move, forgive me. If I beat
time with invisible orchestras, smile with me.
          And I can't even dance.

THE CONDUCTOR

A generosity of water into a sink
pouring and the splashing sounds

falling, falling, like a string
section's soft sighing. My love

conducting with a wooden spoon,
timpanist on the rim of a skillet,

coaxing, urging, enfolding a flame,
gesturing with butter, commanding

with cubes of meat, frizzling,
building to a crescendo of spices

and sauces, and then with the triumph
of completion, turning to me, bowing,

with her face flushed, the fine music
of food, the sweet joy, the living.

THE ARTIST

Who would have thought that it would come to this?
To be enisled in England, liberate
this warm affection without artifice
across from Church? To learn, when separate,

what sharing is? To find, when closest bound,
the need for solitary space? I walk
the upper hall to listen for the sound
of you enhued. Artists are funny folk,

given to lonely cries or sudden mirth.
In the vast cluttered culture where we live
you dig your brush into corrupted earth
for irises to fire your narrative,

or shop the world as one immense bazaar
which I may hope to near, but where you are.

THUNDER EASTWARD

Looking down the slope
over the gray gravestones,
the quiet stones, the everlasting
stones, the banners of death,
you smile as the wild flash
births in cumulus and air
that which will end up here.

Over the combed crowns of willows,
above the Farncombe hill,
the storm passes, moves
ponderously off to call soon
on Kent and Normandy
and bury itself in darker Europe.

But spring forth, sprung life, sweet
from the flowers, your face fair
kissable, your soft skin soothing
fingertips, to glory in flesh,
to meld warm bodies, to
remember. Never mind the days,
the months, the years, with
care, with pain. You watch

the black-creped funerals
and then, with your clear eyes,
turn back to your colors,
to your brushes and your passion.

You have no time for death.

Your mind knows it is alive.
To feel, to think.

You raise your head and listen
as the storm departs for Normandy.

You send its thunder to the east.

A BRIEF HISTORY OF LOVE

I take your willing hand. Your
eyes are echo-chambers,
your pursed lips pattern sounds
that tell me we make sense,
that we are one flesh.
Dragonflies buzz over our heads
and stop. Now they
are mating on our window.
Outside, the tulip tree
flowers like a silent chorus
next to the yew with its
symphony of birdsong.

Our eyes are echo-chambers.
We are the residue of fire,
of a first love created
eons before man, when the dawn air
scented longing
and volcanoes promised heat.

In the beginning, an ordering,
a fulfillment, a coming
together, a one out of two,
an enormous coupling, an anti-
death. In the beginning, life,
a continuum aware of now,
suspecting a future.
A living missile

driving toward today,
toward dragonflies copulating
on our window.

Toward us.

THE QUEEN

She magnifies her corner of the room,
with videos stacked by her royal chair,
a TV at salute, a mass of bloom
to grace the mantle. She governs there,

prepares to hold her court while the BBC
offers an evening menu. Like a Queen
she waves a casual hand and instantly
the cast appears upon a silver screen,

fated to do her bidding. While they dance
and sing she lifts a brimming regal glass
and sips champagne. They tender a romance
in black-and-white, and as a pair embrace

I take her willing hands and bow and crown
her there, royal upon her wicker throne.

THE VIEWER

She sits entranced before the black and white
that flickers from the fabled Hollywood
of Gable, Tracy, Hepburn—at the sight
of the feigned and brittle glamor that she wooed

but never won. Evenings, she sits and sighs
for homage that never was, but might have been,
a meld of mirth and sorrow in her eyes
and on her face a pleasure grown from pain.

And all the while I listen or I watch,
making my music or my stubborn words,
wishing sometimes my clumsy strengths were such
as heroes are made of, wielding mighty swords

to slay real dragons, winning my lady fair
against all odds in bright medieval air.

PROCREATION

With all the pain your life has brought to you
over the years that rest like canvasses done
and stacked haphazardly, with Cerulean Blue
for tragedy, and French Ultramarine

for grief, how is it that you've since become
a sensualist who faces toward the light
and makes a joy of things? In a polychrome
of cadmium red dramatic on zinc white,

of sudden umber, and in hidden deeps
of violet in sea and sky and rocks,
you've made your private world. My lady keeps,
the while she procreates in painting smocks

against all odds and trying circumstance,
a magic multicolored eloquence.

PLEASE LEAVE A PICTURE
OF YOUR LOVE

Fingers of raw and frantic rain,
moments of sleeping sweeted through,
visions of voided lusty love
all from the powerful pound of you.

Why would we mean the who we said?
Was there a language moaned for one?
Manipulate me if you will
but tell me when the rose is gone.

Drunk is the delicate beneath,
dress is the diamond dreaming by,
time is together shadowing,
storm is a thundering of sky.

Day lets no stare be sad nor still.
I know your living will produce
peaches and petals from a tongue
delightfully vociferous.

Please leave a picture of your love
panting a heave above my head.
Sun me a light alive and lie
licking my hot essential blood.

THE OLDER MAN
TO HIS LADY

You have paused above the album with your eye
and I have watched you surreptitiously

and seen the sadness and the lines. You cry
inside because the print shows beautifully

how beautiful she was, the flaming hair, the smile,
the slimness and the curves, that other one, the she

who was your body and your flesh. She who is cruel
by being there. You shift your weight, your thigh

seems cramped, but both of you, the photograph,
the woman sitting in the chair, your mouth,

the rich relaxed abandon of your laugh,
time present and time past, are all the truth,

are all of you, that you, the you I have,
the she who was, who is, the one I love.

IN PRAISE OF FIRE

Your high cheekbones, your Roman nose
capture the light under your red hair.
Why do they make me think of fire?

Imagine a job gone. Being fired.
Imagine warming our throats with gin
and later, on the stove, heating bangers
and mash. Imagine a cigarette.

Alchemy's medieval—but, yes, we
still bow to alchemy: air, water,
earth and fire. Catalyzed by fire,
we cannot live without it. The
lives we live are made with fire.
Our hearts, our minds, consume us
with slow flame. We move as a long
burning in the air enables us,
restores our strength, pulses with
our blood, flushes up our arms
to hold our very love with fire.

And when under stress, and when
rejection comes, the sun a stranger,
the day hopeless and hurtful,
our anger kindles and delivers us.
Our outrage walks on coals. Our fury
fuels us and we slash through the day
in duels with its incendiaries.

Life sears, singes, scorches, scalds.
We spark, we burn, we glow, we smolder
with living. No matter that in time
the years turn to ash, flames go dim—
we will remember, our minds alight.
My pen will move. Your pigments will
cross a virgin canvas, painting
to warm the eyes of a new body
below the sun on an eventual earth.

IMAGINING MY LOVE
DEALING WITH STARS

Remarkable. The dancer
on your music box is the image of
you. Thus I see you twice, and
ghosting through the window
by your bed, a rainbow
insinuating light, to
verify the late sun.

Red is your color, not crimson
or maroon. Under the light
your hair holds copper tones
glowing with Scotland.
But your pasts have gone old.
I join the ranks, declaring
victory. I am your last.

Read above you as you climb
over ridges to the great dome
you work in. Control. Devices
geared to bring down the
barcodes of stars.
In an hour the sky will be
violet. And you will be ready.

Reducing it all to basics:
on your brow I want

yellow, the sun to make it
gold with the evening, and
by morning, convert your
insecure great sparkling
violence into a peace.

Rubies to prism the light?
Or diamonds? Crystal? For
you the sum of these is
greater than all the parts,
being the same as life.
It spells cosmos for you; it
volunteers you for light.

Renascent day rising
out of the east. I thought
you would not expect me here
gray by the green grass,
but you cruise down to me
in your Fiesta, your
valise brimming with stars.

Red is the new sun's color.
Orange tints your lips as
yellow light grows—perfect for
green eyes. Mine are old
blue that watch you sleep as
indigo moves to an intimate
violet that makes it all new.

Red. Orange. Yellow. Green.
Blue. Indigo. Violet.

HUSBANDING

Mornings I begin to fill myself with you:
unlatch the front door, check the heat,
refill your water glass, adjust your chair,
turn on your reading light, become aware
of the notes you've left me in your neat
handwriting, things that I need to do

such as renew a prescription, money for
Sam, post your letters, re-do my grocery list,
add water to a vase of thirsty flowers,
check on the gray sky. Its morning showers
mean no stroll for you. Instead I'll insist
on a daytime film. And meanwhile cram

your happy litter into a waiting bin
and carry it to the kitchen. Up above
I hear a stirring, turn the kettle on,
spoon out coffee into our mugs. Whereupon
your voice comes down. "Ahoy, my love!"
And I go to the foot of the stairs. You grin

at me over the railing, framed by tousled
hair, looking at me with your sleepy drinking
eyes, full of your night's adventures. When I
bring the coffee your slow awakening
centers the day for me. My fingers memorize
your curls, my lips your lips, my air your air.

HOW KIND YOU ARE TO FLOWERS

Your face, this festive evening, glows with light
from two white burning candles. You are dressed
in harvest colors, dear butterfly at night,
and on the table my hungry hands are pressed

on yours, my eyes and ears enslaved. I see
the lilac on your *kaftan*, and its *eau*
gentles the air. You wear it tenderly
and since it breathes the elixir of you

I taste its essence on my thirsty tongue.
I know how kind you are to flowers,
how you thread your fingers among
the roses, and your wordlessness empowers

the silence. Flowers are offerings I make
to kindness. For your sake. For my sake.

AUTONOMY

Sometimes you let me see the pain,
or rather, silent, I surprise it
      clutching at your face,
      forcing you inward,
      until it sees me and retreats
and lets you own yourself again.

The pain is in the rocks you paint
being pummeled by insurgent seas,
      great battering surfs
      roaring in over the gray
      brown bruised granites
of your life. You paint a history.

There is you. There is an outer world.
Something in you prefers it so.
      I have come late to stand
      beside you, and now your hand
      nestles in mine—on your terms—
you of the radiant secret colors.

THE GIFT

Mornings, she works her way down the stairs,
stops at the dining room door, looks in at me.
I rise, enfold and kiss her and, still sleepy, she
snuggles against my shoulder. At first she hears

about my night, then recounts for me her dream
featuring Robert Redford or Stewart Granger
or Nick Nolte or some handsome stranger
who wants a kiss (always a romantic theme),

and I listen and smile and escort her through
to her wicker chair where she spreads her notes
and takes her medicine (my compatriot's
attorney for the defense), then tests the view

through our window. The skies await
the gift of her, sunlit and appropriate.

THE RETURN

And so I've brought her home again
and placed her in her chair to sit
and warm the room. And opposite
I sing my love, my heart, my brain—

and listen to the house. Its sound
is richer, hollow caverns filled
with life, its mantel daffodilled
with flowers that are both profound

and innocent. They have been changed
by pleasing her. The glass reflects
a softness echoing her sex,
the rug's caprice is rearranged,

and all about the room are voice
and face and eyes and counterpoise.

INEBRIATION

Let me manipulate the moon
in my wanting of this woman.
Let me scatter clouds
and father storms.

Let this quiet street grow cool
with shadows, and let me
guide her through the door
and watch her smile.

We music through the evening,
our blood flooding in us.
She lures me with her warmth
and looks a honeyed easy love.

I breathe in her woman
essence, her *eau de vie.*
It's no wonder that I love her;
her eyes cleanse me of ghosts.

THE DOOR

A heavy truck goes by. The door shakes
like a fibrillating heart, hesitates,
echoes down the hall, pulls me through
into a further room precisely where
her helplessness is on display. I stand
beside her rumpled bed, trying to smile.
The stillness holds a ragged breath, her
searching eyes catch mine to reinforce
her need of me. Here there be viruses,
silent thieves that take no note of love.

I say the usual things to her. I touch
her hand, make gestures of solicitude.
"Ice water, love?" "Another pillow, love?"
"Five people have come by!" I shape
her air with my reportage. Lightly I talk
of future holidays, of cruises we must
plan. Does she recall the B and B
in Hanover? Living over a kitchen
in Positano? Treading wooden planks
above the flooded squares of Venice?

I pour myself a glass of wine, dip in
a finger, touch it to her lips. She winks
a toast to me, I raise my glass to her.
Here's to you, Sweetheart . . . your singing
arteries, your metered mouth, your
great receptacles of eyes. We strange

creatures: only when our fires are mostly ash
to learn what fire is. How ripeness glows.
How often have we scanned a crowded room
to find her hair, her face, her eyes, our love.

The door has gently closed. Her voice
converts the room into a history,
the nudes upon the wall, the table rich
with paints, the waiting canvasses.
She talks the art alive and teaches me
rainbows of color. She seems to grow
from layered oils, each of her works
a rich tableaux, as if the brushes
wrote her moments, the daubs her days,
the canvasses her years, the all her life.

DECEMBER POEM

It feels—in grim December—that Spring may not
come again. That there's no sun to melt
the snow scuffed by our heavy shoes. How can
we wind the clock of warmer seasons when
the drift is piled around us? But we are here
as lovers, and I propose that we not fear
this month of endings. Even these frosted hours
promise a festival and Christmas flowers.

And so the winter broods. For all the years
that stir in plastic memory, the stares,
the smiles, you with your Queenly eyes,
me with my grateful grin, I would propose
a song centering on a cold December
trembling at year's end, to remember
flowers on a dying day. We feel
a frozen earth unable to reveal

that tulips will be coloring the Spring,
but they will come. There is always morning
after evening. Even in this cold Park
a night bird sings. A man and woman walk
with roses over the icy street and sit
upon our empty wooden bench. Is that
how our December ends? From what I see
she is your likeness, and he could be me.

WALKING ALONE

I cut through Peperharow, find a footpath
snaking through woods, thick up to the right,
scattered down to the left toward the river.

Tracing its casual curves, I feel the bones
in my thighs stretch, think of her at home,
and feel the mobile in my pocket. Ahead,

as the path mounts a small rise, I catch
movement and stop, stand motionless while
a cock pheasant turns and pecks the ground

and preens. This is what she would love,
and I gaze intensely. I must carry it back
to her with words: pheasant, earth, woods,

blue sky, sun, breeze, the bursting feel
of May. She will sit captive in her chair
and have me spell it out, she who would

once amble here, stroll, swing along without
aim or goal, cry out at the yellow butterfly,
caress her face with bluebells. She who

would picnic with me at the foot of the oak,
laughing across the pasture at the black
horses, chewing excitedly on her tuna

mayo. She who would point at the Lab,
golden in the sun, that stops and looks back
for its determined brown-haired mistress

who marches past with kit bag and staff.
"Now who do you think she is?" My lady
would say. "Secretary? No, too cocky.

Clerk? Ditto. Teacher? Maybe. And alone.
Hmmm. Smart enough to own a dog."
And so the story would build. She would

spin chapters as we munch our sandwiches,
and I would be willing captive of her art.
For her the people we meet or see,

the earth, the passing days, are rich
and flavorful. "Like chocolates!" she cries.
"Sometimes meaty! Sometimes crunchy!

Sometimes soft-cored! Sometimes ugh!"
At home she watches me as I talk,
her eyes drinking in the second-hand

sunlight, the postcard oak, the painted
hill. She brings a palette out of me
rich with word colors I did not know I knew.